This book is dedicated to
June Burke and Julian,
my teachers

Transformational Meditation

CONTENTS

1.	Preface	....	3
2.	Introduction	....	4
3.	Let's Meditate	....	10
	Balancing Meditation	....	10
4.	Levels of Consciousness	....	16
5.	A Guided Meditation	....	22
	Forest Meditation	....	22
6.	Transformation	....	26
7.	Our Chakra System	....	30
	Root	....	34
	Sacral	....	36
	Solar Plex	....	38
	Heart	....	40
	Throat	....	44
	Brow	....	46
	Crown	....	48
8.	Meditation with Chakras	....	53
	Seven Chakra Meditation	....	53
9.	Using Chakra Meditations	....	58
	Bicycle Meditation	....	58
	Problem Solving Meditation	....	60
10.	Handling Transformations	....	64
	Overcoming Sadness	....	68
	Establishing Proper Thoughts	....	70
	Handling Embarrassments	....	71
	Handling Anger	....	73
11.	Can I Go Higher?	....	78
	Astral	....	82
	White Plateau	....	84
	Nine Chakra Meditation	....	85
12.	What's Next?	....	88

ILLUSTRATIONS

1.	Balancing Meditation	....	9
2.	Levels of Consciousness	....	15
3.	Forest Meditation	....	21
4.	Seven Chakras	....	29
5.	Root	....	33
6.	Sacral	....	35
7.	Solar Plexus	....	37
8.	Heart	....	39
9.	Throat	....	43
10.	Brow	....	45
11.	Crown	....	47
12.	Discovery	....	51
13.	Integration	....	52
14.	Bicycle Meditation	....	57
15.	Handling Transformation	....	63
16.	Nine Chakras	....	77
17.	Astral	....	81
18.	White Plateau	....	83
19.	Self Transformation	....	87

PREFACE

Sooner or later we feel compelled to do something that eases the emotional pain we experience as part of everyday life. We feel compelled to find something that will give us direction that is irrefutable in its truth. We feel a strong urge to do whatever it takes to enrich our lives. It doesn't matter what the risks are, there is a compelling desire to put everything that drags us down and holds us back aside and get on with our lives.

I came to that point in my life in 1973. It was then that I discovered the joy of meditation. I knew deep within myself that meditation was the key. I knew that if I was to survive difficult changes in my life and grow spiritually I needed to meditate. I knew with certainty that if I was to handle the changes that were before me I had to meditate.

Well, I don't know if you feel as strongly about meditation as that. However, I do. This book represents what I have learned and experienced about meditation over these last years. My desire is that meditation will help you on your unique journey. Good luck!

INTRODUCTION

I remember one time when I had been puzzling at length about how I should align priorities concerning teaching meditation and managing projects at my highly technical job. On one hand, I derived a great sense of fulfillment from teaching. On the other hand, I loved my technical career and I felt that I could make significant contributions. The working environment was intense and required considerable attention, leaving me little time and energy for teaching. I could see no way to pursue both aspects simultaneously. I needed both in my life, or at least I thought I did.

One morning I woke up feeling as if a great problem had been resolved. When I got to work my boss called me in and said that he would like me to increase my focus on a particular aspect of my job. That aspect was the part that I felt the greatest affinity for, and was also the easiest to handle from a pressure point-of-view. Of course I accepted the change of direction. Later the same day, I was talking to a friend about my new priorities and he said that his project was just completed and he would like to help. His participation in the project allowed even less stress on my part. In short, my work became easier and more fulfilling without sacrificing my career. I had plenty of time and energy to pursue teaching meditation.

I attribute that beneficial change to my practice of meditation and the transformation it brings. In other instances I found far more mundane joys that clearly seemed to arise after I began to meditate. I found rush hour traffic easier to cope with and parking places easier to find. I no longer found myself getting upset if others express opinions that are different from mine. Things just seemed to happen with less fuss and bother. I no longer feel as if I am pushing against a river. I've changed my attitude from one of resistance and hassle to one of acceptance and joy using meditation as the facilitator. My life has changed for the better.

This is an aspect of meditation (at least the type of meditation that is being presented here) that is most beautiful. Meditation will often take you through a change you will not be aware of until it is complete. You will wake up some morning and say, "Boy! I feel better. It's as if a weight has been lifted! What happened?" Well, what's happened is that the truth and wisdom found in meditation has taken you from point A to point B without any conscious intervention on your part. Your wise inner self has put you there without any struggle or conscious work on your part.

A very wise friend once told me that the path to all enlightenment was through meditation. At that time I knew what my friend said was true. I can't explain why I knew, but I knew I had experienced truth. Perhaps you have experienced the same feeling sometime in the past: a shiver runs up and down your spine or the hairs on your arm seem to stand up and you get goose bumps. It's a wonderful feeling. It is a signal that emanates from the greatest aspect of your inner self. It comes from that part of you that is wise enough to recognize truth. In this instance, the part of me that knows great truth let me know that what I heard was important. It got my attention through a physical sensation. That physical sensation gave me a tremendous feeling of well being. I experienced an inner joy with my discovery of truth!

Meditation helps us in many aspects of our life. Many people are drawn to meditation because there are so many hassles in their lives that they need an outlet. They need to create a space so that peace of mind can enter. Have you ever met or experienced a person who seems to have such strong inner peace that it rubs off on you? Has someone entered a room full of chaotic or argumentative people and by their very touch or presence quieted the situation? These people may or may not consciously be meditators, but their nature is meditative. They bring with them the quality of inner peace found in meditation.

Meditation also allows transformations to occur. If our lives are to become enriched movement must take place. Movement means that we need to revaluate our current position and accept change that will take us to a better position. Yes, we must change! We must transform an existing frame of reference to a new and better one. Meditation helps these transformations in three ways: It allows you to see that change is necessary if growth is to happen. It allows you to see what change will be most beneficial, and it helps you through the change in a gentle and supportive manner.

Meditation allows truth, peace, and beneficial transformation in our lives. If you really want these things, it is time to seriously take a look at and experience meditation. Accept those things that ring true for you. Meditation has been a great enrichment in my life and is now a beneficial part of my life that will never diminish and will never leave me. I would like it to be the catalyst that brings great enrichment into your life. I know of no better way to share it with you than through this book about meditation.

Transformational Meditation

Balancing Meditation

LET'S MEDITATE

Balancing Meditation

There's nothing complicated about meditation. It is a natural state of being, a state that everyone can achieve as easily as breathing.

In fact, a first meditation, one you can do right now, is to **sit comfortably, close your eyes and take three deep breaths. Just sit calmly without any expectations. Don't worry about your posture or about your thoughts. Be free of preconceived notions of what will happen. If you have to scratch your nose, move your legs, etc., go ahead and do it. It won't disturb the meditation and it is best to get it out of the way sooner than later. Simply sit down, close your eyes and take three deep breaths.**

That's all!

Now, lets talk about what happened. (You did do it, didn't you? If not, take two minutes and do it now. The rest of what you read will make more sense.)

Meditation is allowing the physical body to take care of itself while the mind naturally moves beyond mundane thoughts. That's what happened during the previous meditation.

Sitting quietly and comfortably put the body at ease. As you closed your eyes you removed the bulk of the external stimuli you normally experience in a non-meditative state. Removing external stimuli allows you to experience a higher, more inward level of consciousness. Finally, as you took three deep breaths, two things happened: First, your body relaxed further and its automatic process of taking care of itself became an easier task. Second, more oxygen entered your system. This helps the mind to rise to a higher level of consciousness.

Look back at how you felt before the meditation and how you felt immediately following it. It's natural for you to become more relaxed and at peace. Some people feel a slight tingling, usually in their hands. But, in any case, whether you felt anything or not, you meditated!

Let's look at the process in a little more depth. You want to avoid distractions if possible. Distractions tend to take your mind back to mundane thoughts and make it difficult for you to become balanced. Being physically comfortable in meditation is important. Some people prefer to sit on a chair, while others like a cushion or the floor. It's helpful to find a position that keeps your back reasonably straight as this allows more comfortable and deeper meditations. Your sitting posture (in particular the straightness of the back) will become more important in the future as you continue to meditate. Don't be overly concerned about it now. You will naturally move to a position and posture that is best for you.

Some people prefer to meditate lying down. This may work well for them. However, when I try to meditate in that position I usually go to sleep! (That's OK when I need sleep. However, sleep is not meditation. In meditation the mind rises in consciousness; in sleep the mind goes to sleep. Two very different levels of consciousness, both of them important.)

The three deep breaths are equally important. Try this brief exercise: put one hand over the upper part of your chest and the other hand just above your belly button. Now take a few deep breaths and notice whether one hand is pushed outward more than the other. If the answer is yes, one part of your lungs is receiving more oxygen than the other and so you're not completely filling your lungs. This means that your body is not receiving as much oxygen as it could.

Many of us tend to be shallow breathers. We tend to be concerned about the way we look and, consequently, hold our tummies in. This results in unfilled lungs. Remember, oxygen is important. Later, when we get into another form of meditation, the oxygen will help your clarity of consciousness.

The deep breathing will also bring your body into balance. While you are breathing in, envision peace and harmony entering. When you are breathing out, visualize cares or worries leaving. This will bring a deeper state of relaxation and give you a greater sense of inward well-being.

Work with this exercise for awhile until you're comfortable with the way you are breathing.

I would suggest that you practice the first meditation (the balancing meditation) a few times until the process becomes second nature and you no longer need be concerned with the process. Sometimes it will seem as if the meditation is deeper than other times. This is normal and you need not worry about it. Just accept your experience as it is, and know that progress is always taking place.

If random thoughts enter (for instance, "Did I put the cat out?" or "I hope that I locked the door") handle them by quietly but firmly saying to yourself, "That thought is not a part of this meditation. I put it aside." With practice, random thoughts will be few and far between.

Many thoughts that come in meditation are fine. In fact, much of the benefit in meditation stems from that type of interaction. It is normal for us to be curious: we want to know how to improve our lives and continue our spiritual enrichment. The key is to allow only those thoughts to enter your meditation that come from a point of truth.

Well, you now are an experienced meditator. I'm not joking! You now have the basic skills for meditation. You can stop here and just do this meditation as often as you like. Ultimately, whatever else you need will come in its own time. However, if you, like me, are curious and a bit impatient, it may not be time to put this book aside. Wonderful worlds of inner transformation and understanding are to be achieved quite rapidly if you are persistent.

Transformational Meditation

Three Levels of Consciousness

LEVELS OF CONSCIOUSNESS

When you meditate you ascend through levels of consciousness.

In reality, consciousness is a continuum with an infinite number of levels. Each of the different levels of consciousness have their own rate of vibration. The lower levels have a slow vibration, while the higher levels have a more rapid vibration. We experience these different levels as we meditate.

The lower vibratory rates are just as important as the higher ones. There is no level of consciousness that is best or even better that any other. All levels are useful and have value when meditation is used to facilitate growth.

In order to cope with the infinite levels of consciousness, meditative tradition divides them into three main levels. These levels relate to the way the mind views and works with any aspect of our lives. The levels are the conscious mind, the subconscious mind, and the superconscious mind. It is useful to understand what each level means and how it's used so you can recognize and work with it.

Conscious Mind

The lowest level is the conscious mind. We use it to decide what we want to accomplish and how to accomplish it. The conscious mind works within the framework of logic (at least, we would like to think so).

Your conscious mind is based upon your culture, upbringing, genetic structure, and view of the world. Your conscious mind is logical and deterministic. It is the aspect of your mind through which personality and ego are expressed.

The conscious mind determines what is good and bad and therefore is concerned with moral issues. Have you ever tried to get a even small group of people to decide how a moral issue should be handled? If so, you probably spent most of the time trying to define what was morally correct. There are usually as many points of view as there are individuals in the discussion.

Subconscious Mind

The middle level is the subconscious mind. The subconscious mind operates at a higher vibratory level than the conscious mind. Surprised? Many people view the subconscious mind as the lower, animalistic part of ourselves. That part is actually the lowest aspect of the conscious mind.

The subconscious deals with two things: the control of the physical body, and memory. The subconscious controls and regulates our heartbeat, breathing, release of adrenaline, etc. It is associated with the pituitary gland and the automatic nervous system. The subconscious mind is also the storage area for everything we have ever experienced through the senses (seeing, hearing, touching, smelling, or tasting). It is like a computer memory bank. It does not put a value on anything it remembers. It just remembers the "facts."

There's nothing in the subconscious mind that judges events as right or wrong. Everything is remembered equally. It is the conscious mind that judges. The subconscious mind is influenced by repetition and emotion. The stronger the emotion or the more often the thought is repeated, the stronger the impression within the subconscious mind.

Superconscious Mind

The third and highest level of consciousness is the superconscious mind. The superconscious mind always knows what is right. Does that sound odd? Indeed, there is a part of us that always knows truth. There is a part of us that always knows what is best.

Transformational Meditation

That part of us is the superconscious. It can be experienced and contacted in meditation. The superconscious mind also speaks to us through dreams and intuition. We must be very still to hear the quiet, gentle voice of our superconscious mind. The need of the superconscious mind to communicate in quietness is the fundamental reason for meditation.

Some time back I lost my car keys and had a very difficult time finding them. Finally, in utter exasperation, I said "I give up." I released my immediate need to locate my keys and decided I would have another set made. I sat down with a great sigh. When I got up a short time later, I wandered into the corner of my kitchen. I looked down near the waste basket and picked up my keys! I suspect that everyone can remember a similar instance that has happened to them.

When I gave up, sat down, and allowed myself the release of a deep breath, a wonderful thing happened. A spontaneous state similar to meditation occurred. I wasn't aware of it at the time but it was meditation nonetheless. During that instant of quiet release, the superconscious mind communicated to the subconscious mind where my keys were. The superconscious mind knew that it was best for me to find the keys, because I was on my way to a meeting that was to be formulative in my growth process.

The subconscious mind knew where the keys were and it controlled the physical body. It was then just a matter of the subconscious mind getting me off of my backside and over to the car keys.

That little story is a perfect example of how the levels of our mind interact. When the conscious mind is too busy or too noisy to allow the subtlety of the superconscious mind to be heard, the superconscious will impress the information upon the subconscious mind to be released at the proper time. You can hear the superconscious directly during the quietness of meditation. Meditation is the direct path to superconscious thought. Meditation is where we receive information that is true and beneficial for our growth. So meditate! It's worth it!

It does take some practice to separate superconscious information from the mundane activities of the conscious mind, but it can be done. If the voice you hear is loud or judgmental, it is the conscious mind. If you think that certain information has come from your superconscious, follow it. If it turns out to be a blind alley or undesirable, then chalk it up to the conscious mind. If it brings an unexpected benefit or growth, attribute it to the superconscious. It won't take long for you to acquire the skill required to tell them apart. Keep in mind that the superconscious mind is quiet, gentle, and never expresses judgement.

Transformational Meditation

The Forest Meditation

A GUIDED MEDITATION

I would like to share with you a meditation that I have been using for many years. It's easy to follow and remember. This is a meditation that has always brought a sense of peace and well being within me. In addition, this meditation provides a foundation that will be helpful as further meditations are introduced. I use it when I have had (or, for that matter, know I will have) a particularly trying day. You can easily guide yourself through it. It is called the Forest Meditation.

Forest Meditation

The meditation begins by doing the first meditation (the Balancing Meditation) described in this book. **Get into a comfortable position. Close your eyes. Take three deep breaths, drawing in peace and harmony as you breath in and expelling cares and worries as you breath out. Now, inwardly sense the well being and balance you have achieved.**

Next, imagine yourself in the midst of a deep forest. There is complete stillness and quiet in that forest. In the depths of the forest there is comfort and strength. Feel yourself becoming a part of the forest.

After you have become comfortable in the forest, sense a path stretching out before you. As you move along the path you come to a large, quiet pond. Sit down, or if you would like, wade into the pond and sense its cool, refreshing water. Drop a pebble into its center. Feel the rhythm and timing of the concentric circles spreading out from the place where you dropped the pebble. Become a part of the water and feel its creative energies.

Move gently beyond the pond and sense before you a large, open meadow. As you move into the meadow there is a feeling of warmth from the sun above. Perhaps you can sense the sounds and rapid movement of insects and animals that inhabit the meadow. You sense the vitality of the movement and it has a calming effect on you. You become one with the warmth of the sun and an inner understanding of yourself emerges. You feel happy to be alive.

Looking up from the meadow, you sense a tall mountain and are instantly drawn into its foothills. The mountain air is refreshing. As you take a deep breath, it has a cleansing effect. It makes you feel lighter and gives you a great sense of freedom.

In this freedom you move quickly and easily up to the top of the mountain. You can stay on top for as long as you like. On this mountaintop, you can experience any and all things because you have gone beyond all physical boundaries. You have the freedom to be who you really are.

After you spend some time on the mountaintop, you decide it is time to return. On your way down it is important to revisit the foothills, to feel their rarified air, to sense the meadow and feel its warmth, to pause by the pond and feel its creative refreshment, to reenter the forest and feel its quiet strength. Now make a conscious effort to feel the earth beneath you and return from the meditation.

Become familiar with the Forest Meditation through practice. It will be a great help in the meditations that follow. Read over the steps a number of times. Remember that your subconscious will know it by heart instantly, but it is helpful for your conscious mind to understand it also. When you are practicing this meditation, all you need to do is to think of the forest or the other places you will visit. The thought alone is enough to take you there. I have found it useful to remember a particularly nice grove of trees that I have physically visited in the past, or a pond that I found appealing during my childhood. The memory of the physical places will help you to experience them more inwardly in mediation.

Each person has their own way of sensing things, of experiencing things internally. Some people visualize easily, seeing things in mental images. Others have an inner feeling that creates an awareness of what they are sensing. Still others hear sounds clearly or smell the scents of the forest, and so on. Notice how you perceive. Become familiar with your own unique way of inner perception. The important thing to remember is to observe your own awareness of the places you visit in this meditation, and how your awareness becomes part of the quality of the environment.

TRANSFORMATION

The answer to that age old question, "Why am I here?" is: To grow as much as possible. Growth means movement. Movement means change. Change means transformation. Transformation -- that's what it's all about! If meditation is to benefit you, it must help you move from where you are now to a better state. But, what is better? Where are you now? Where do you want to go? Will it hurt? These are all great questions, and you must answer them for yourself with the utmost care and wisdom.

After years of counseling I have noticed that there is no universally right answer. What is right for one person is not appropriate for another. Each person is unique, the result of a complex mixture of culture, upbringing, environment, and individual needs and desires. Each individual has unique growth patterns, each with its own timing. Ultimately, you must choose the path that best fits your needs. This means that each individual must set into motion ideas and activities that bring growth into their life. Or, looking at it in another way, you must be responsible for your own transformation.

All that's well and good. However, we know that at times change can be painful, and we can be reluctant to face it. I can be as stubborn and set in my ways as anyone, and in the past I've sometimes needed to be hit over the head with a cosmic ball bat in order to be dislodged from my position so I could change and move on.

Through years of lots of change, though, I've learned to trust my higher self and accept change at its face value. I know that my meditations put me in the frame of reference that will bring change into my life as I need it.

Astounding isn't it? When I learned to trust my higher self, I also gave myself permission to help direct change so I could grow! Indeed, I found that change, and the resultant growth, was fun. I found joy in seeing the results of each episode of change. In addition, and perhaps most importantly, I found that the cosmic ball bat was no longer needed. The change I experienced was gentle and fulfilling.

If we place our transformation under the guidance of our highest self, our superconscious, we can't loose. After all, our superconscious is always right, isn't it? Direct contact with our superconscious is possible in meditation. Meditation -- that's the bottom line!

When we meditate, we raise our consciousness through many levels to the superconscious. This act in itself is a transformation as we move our mental state from its conscious level to its superconscious level. As we listen to our superconscious mind, and act upon what we learn, its wisdom enriches our lives. We transform our present condition to a better state. We grow in the right direction.

Meditation will teach you to trust in your higher self. The trust is a catalyst for the superconscious to direct change in your life so that you experience positive growth. The growth will be timely and positive. Your superconscious will do it no other way.

We have talked about the mental transformation that occurs in meditation, and the transformation this allows in your life. Now it's time to quit talking about it and do it! We'll work through meditations that are directed through an internal system of energy centers, called "chakras."

Transformational Meditation

The Seven Chakras

OUR CHAKRA SYSTEM

Chakras are energy centers, or vortices of energy. There are seven major chakras located within your physical body. The seven chakras are unequally spaced starting at the base of your spine and ending at the top of your head. I will describe these chakras in some detail because transformational meditation deals chiefly with them.

Quite a lot has been written about chakras from many different perspectives. In this book I would like to help you understand them by direct experience of their essence. Their essence energies are extremely helpful in understanding yourself. It is self understanding that rests at the heart of growth and transformation.

Each chakra has an unique rate of vibration. The chakra that is lowest in your body, the root chakra at the base of your spine, has the slowest rate of vibration. The crown chakra at the top of your head has the fastest.

The rate of increase in vibration is not the same between the chakras. The increase in vibratory rate between the lower four chakras is much smaller than between the upper three. You will find it much easier to physically relate to the lower four chakras because they deal with the physical, or more elemental, aspects of yourself. The upper three chakras deal chiefly with the spiritual realms and have less correspondence with the physical world.

Each chakra spins, creating a spiralling pattern. The spin alternates from chakra to chakra, a clockwise spiral and then a counterclockwise spiral. The spiraling pattern expresses active and receptive energies: a clockwise spiral is active while a counterclockwise spiral is receptive. Active and receptive patterns of the chakras alternate in accordance with their spin and, when necessary, reverse. The directional change is subtle and normally you won't notice it.

There is a color associated with each chakra. Just as the chakras are in order from the slowest vibration to the highest vibration, their corresponding colors move from lowest frequency to highest frequency. The first chakra is red, the second orange, the third yellow, the fourth green, the fifth light blue, the sixth indigo blue, and the seventh violet. The chakra colors follow the colors of the rainbow.

Each chakra has a sense associated with it. The first chakra has the sense of smell, the second taste, the third sight, the fourth touch, the fifth speech, the sixth knowledge, and the seventh wisdom. Note that the sense of knowledge and wisdom extend beyond what is normally considered the five senses. You will quickly be able to relate to these "higher" senses as you practice the meditative forms that use the chakras.

The chakras, whether the four elemental ones or the three spiritual ones, are of equal value and are equally necessary for our understanding, transformation, and growth. One chakra is not better than another. In time you will be able to associate with and use all of them equally.

Let's get on with a description of each chakra so you can understand its use and value in meditation. Allow yourself to experience each chakra as you read its description. The experience will arise as a result of sensing the energy and attributes described, whether this be through visualization or inner feelings. The depth of your understanding will be directly proportional to your inner sense of the chakra. Outer, or intellectual, understanding is less important.

Transformational Meditation

The Root Chakra

The Elemental Chakras

The four lower chakras are elemental in nature. They correspond to the elements earth, water, fire, and air, as described by the ancient alchemist. This does not invalidate the periodic table of the elements defined by our modern physicists. Far from it. These four elements provide a simple yet profound way to describe physical and emotional properties. Remember that your inner sense (the internal feeling) of the chakras is important.

The Root Chakra

The first chakra is called the root chakra and is located at the very base of the spine. It corresponds to the elemental qualities of earth; the density of earthy things such as soil, rocks, and trees. Do you remember the deep forest from the Forest Meditation? You were relating to the earth element and the root chakra then.

The root chakra is a place of solidity and strength. You can experience absolute stillness there, a complete lack of movement. It provides a feeling of comfort -- almost a womb-like quality. The color of the root chakra is a deep vibrant red. The dense bones, cartilage, and muscles of your body are all representative of the root. The sense of smell can

Transformational Meditation

The Sacral Chakra

become particularly acute as you focus on the root chakra. It's as if you can smell the damp earth beneath you. At the root chakra you can feel yourself rooting into the earth like a large tree.

The Sacral Chakra

The second chakra is called the sacral chakra. It is located a couple of inches above and in front of the root chakra. This chakra is associated with the elemental qualities of water. Remember the pond in the Forest Meditation? The pond, as water, is associated with the sacral chakra.

The color of the sacral chakra is a glowing orange. Its elemental quality is that of water. The sacral chakra relates to creative flow. There is a gentle movement here that creates rhythm and a flow. It's like the waves and tides of the ocean: a quiet movement that can have tremendous force behind it. Remember, that water also exists as a gentle mist or a powerful rain storm. The sacral chakra can have all of those properties, but underlying them is creativity, rhythm, and flow.

The sacral chakra corresponds to the fluids of the body including blood, saliva, and semen. The sacral chakra is the seat of creative desire. Every act of creation you engage in stems from the sacral chakra. This includes such things as writing, singing,

Transformational Meditation

The Solar Plexus Chakra

cooking, working, and procreation. You will also find that the sense of taste is intensified as you focus on the sacral chakra. Please don't rush by the beauty of the sacral chakra! Creation and joy are closely coupled. Experience the great sense of joy that comes with any creative activity.

The Solar Plexus Chakra

The third chakra is located about one inch below and just behind the belly button. It is called the solar plexus chakra and corresponds to the elemental qualities of fire. As you relate back to the Forest Meditation, the warmth of the meadow corresponds to fire and to the solar plexus chakra.

The fire element is represented in your body as the nervous system. Fire can be the soft glow of a candle or the roaring movement of a forest fire. In its purest form it is electrical in nature and corresponds to lightning. Its color is a brilliant yellow.

The sense of hearing is amplified as you focus upon the solar plexus chakra. The solar plexus is the seat of introspection and inner knowing. It is the source of your gut feel. (In ancient times, people thought their minds were located in the solar plexus. They used gut-level intuition to survive.) When you get butterflies before you meet a person or before you make a public speech, it's your solar plexus talking.

Transformational Meditation

The Heart Chakra

The introspective-you is apprehensive about how the meeting will turn out and the solar plexus responds accordingly.

> The elemental qualities of fire have a rapid movement. However, the rapid movement has a balancing effect. When the solar plexus is balanced there is an inward feeling of well being. There is pride in knowing yourself. Don't be apprehensive about a close look into the inner world of the solar plexus. You will like the you that is to be found there!

The Heart Chakra

The fourth and last elemental chakra is located in the center of your chest just behind your breastbone. It is called the heart chakra and its color is bright green. It is associated with the elemental qualities of air, the lightest of the elements.

The lightness of the heart chakra corresponds to the pulmonary system of the body, the exchange of air in the lungs and the oxygen carried by the blood. Air and the heart chakra have an expansive quality about them. The heart chakra corresponds to the lightness found in the foothills in the Forest Meditation.

The sense of touch is amplified as you focus on the heart chakra. It is the quality of the heart chakra that allows you to reach out and sense, or touch, something or someone that is beyond your physical reach. It is not by chance that the heart is associated with love. Love reaches out and touches others. I love you. It has a great feeling to it, doesn't it?

It is through the heart chakra that we understand the environment around us and that the environment understands us. While the solar plexus is the seat of inner understanding, the heart is the seat of external understanding. The heart chakra has a beautiful sense of freedom and expansive joy about it. Its lightness allows you to touch all that is beneficial within the environment around you. Experience the expansion, understanding, and love of the heart chakra.

Those are the elemental chakras. Now onward and upward to the remaining three.

The Nonelemental Chakras

The three remaining chakras have no direct elemental counterpart in the physical world. They are beyond the physical. This does not mean they are better. Your balance needs the trinity of the physical, mental, and spiritual realms for complete understanding and transformation. The nonelemental chakras correspond to the mountaintop in the Forest Meditation. Let's get right into them. Each is intriguing in its own way.

Transformational Meditation

The Throat Chakra

The Throat Chakra

The fifth chakra, the throat chakra, is located directly behind the Adam's Apple. Its color is light sky blue. This chakra is a bridge between the physical world (including the elemental chakras) and everything that is beyond the physical, both mental and spiritual. As a bridge it is associated with communication, particularly spoken communication. The sense associated with the throat chakra is speech. Spoken communication bridges your thoughts (your mind) to others.

The throat chakra is also the place where time and space are formed. Sounds esoteric doesn't it? You can focus on the throat chakra, sense its energy, and be cognizant of the physical world below, yet also be aware of the spiritual world above. You can be aware of time but also you can move beyond the constraint of time.

The throat chakra is where your personality begins to disappear, yet there is still a strong awareness of your individuality. In other words, that part of your personality that is negative begins to give way to your higher self that knows how perfect you already are. The throat chakra is incredibly useful. Experiencing its energy allows you to sense how to bridge truth found in the spiritual world into your physical life.

Transformational Meditation

The Brow Chakra

The Brow Chakra

The sixth chakra is called the brow chakra. It is located just above the bridge of your nose, in the center of your forehead. The brow chakra is sometimes called the third eye. The color of the brow chakra is deep indigo blue.

This chakra is associated with knowledge and the mind. The mind is the originator of all physical manifestation. If you take a close look at anything that has come into your life, you will find that it has been preceded by associated thoughts. It is the seat of understanding, of knowledge. All knowledge can be brought into a form that is understood at the brow chakra. If it seems that this description is a bit nebulous it is because the energy of the brow chakra is nebulous. The brow chakra can reach beyond the conscious mind's need to understand, into the realm of intuitive wisdom where the energy of pure, undirected thought can be experienced.

Transformational Meditation

The Crown Chakra

The Crown Chakra

The seventh and last chakra is called the crown chakra. It is located in the center of the top of your head. Its colors are swirling shades of violet and purple. The crown chakra is associated with the sense of wisdom. This chakra is the portal to all that is beyond physical need and understanding. It is the portal to the universal mind. The universal mind is all knowing and all wise. It is the seat of all that ever was, is, or will be.

The crown chakra corresponds to the highest mountain peak in the Forest Meditation. It is the point of departure of all self-centered aspects of our physical world. It is where universal knowledge enters.

The crown chakra must be experienced in order to understand it. It is beyond conscious comprehension. It is beyond the conscious mind's ability to analyze. Your experience of the energy of the crown chakra will often be an inner understanding without a clear conscious knowledge of what it is that you understand. Actually this can be comforting. Think of it -- knowledge without the time consuming need to understand.

You will find that all experiences found within the energy of the crown chakra eventually will become consciously used. The use comes when the need arises. Experiencing the crown chakra can make you feel spacy. The crown chakra is well beyond the physical world.

That covers all seven chakras. Thanks for sticking with it. Now, let's see how you can use the seven chakras in meditation. This is where the benefit really begins.

Transformational Meditation

**Chakra Meditation
Discovery**

Chakra Meditation

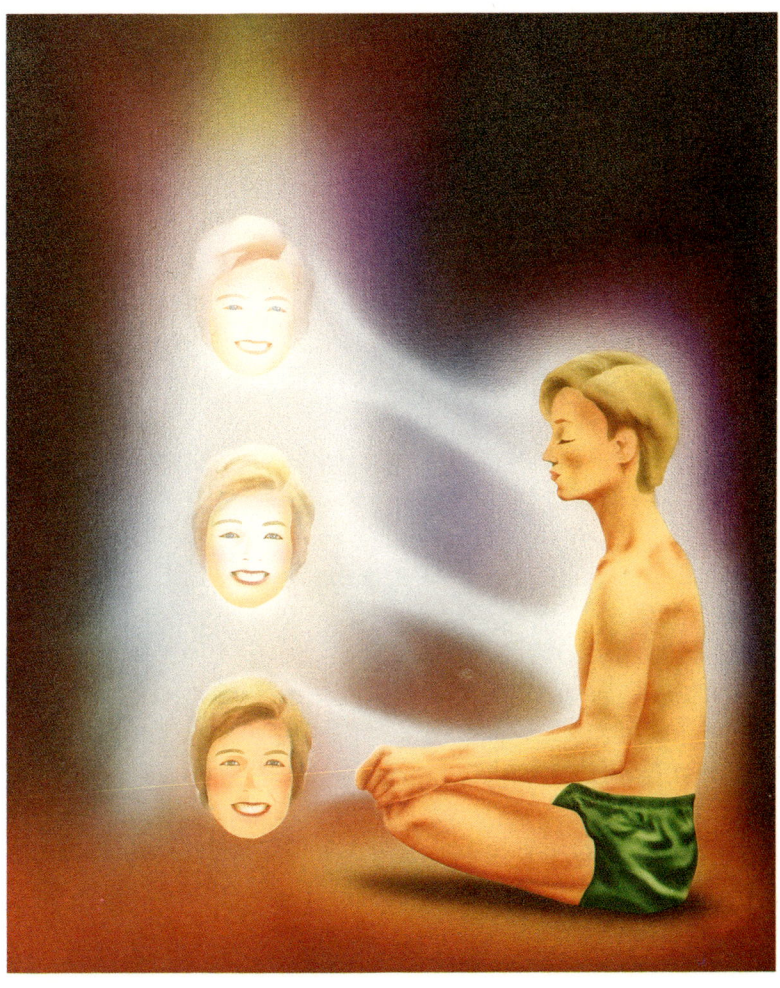

**Chakra Meditation
Integration**

MEDITATION WITH THE CHAKRAS

Meditation with the chakras means spending time focused on each chakra, experiencing each chakra and the energies it represents. This is accomplished simply by focusing your attention at the physical location of each chakra in turn. As you become focused, you experience that chakras energy and its relationship to you. If you really want to understand what you're all about, meditate with the chakras. How? Let's see.

You have noticed by now the similarity between each part of the Forest Meditation and the individual chakras. Below is a guided meditation with the chakras. It begins just like the Forest Meditation.

Chakra Meditation

First relax, close your eyes, and take three deep breaths. Envision yourself balanced and at ease.

Next, focus on each chakra, one at a time, starting at the root chakra and proceeding up to the crown chakra.

Pause awhile at each chakra to sense its properties and its corresponding representation within

yourself. This sense can be enhanced by visualizing yourself merging with the elemental quality of the chakra: earth for the first chakra, water for the second chakra, fire for the third chakra, air for the fourth chakra, the bridging of the fifth chakra, the mind of the sixth chakra, and the universe of the seventh chakra. If you are oriented toward colors, visualizing the colors will help. If you are visually oriented, seeing the elemental qualities as you did in the Forest Meditation will help. If you are a feeling person, allow yourself to internally touch the elemental aspects. Read through the descriptions of the chakras a number of times until you become familiar with them.

A literal interpretation is not necessary. Simply sense the energy and the experience of each chakra. The experience will be different for each person. You are unique, you know.

Finally, beginning at the crown chakra, step back down through all chakras including the root. Consciously feel the density of the earth and gently open your eyes.

The last step is important. Don't skip it! If you come back immediately from the crown chakra you will be spacy. Re-entry into the physical world without the intermediate steps can be disorienting. I wouldn't want you to walk into walls or such.

Become familiar with all seven chakras. Experientially learn them through practicing the Chakra Meditation. As time goes on you will be able to go up and down through each chakra smoothly. It will only take a minute or so. Initially however, spend time at each chakra on the way up and way down until you have an inner sense and feeling of the energy of each chakra.

Your energy and atunement will rev up as you move upward through the chakras, and return to normal as you step back down through the chakras. It is somewhat like shifting a car up and down through its gears. Don't skip chakras! Each one is important. If you feel exceptionally spacy at the end of the meditation, it means you have not spent enough time with the lower four elemental chakras on the way back down from the crown chakra. It is a good idea to go back and revisit the lower four chakras. In addition, feeling the density of the earth or feeling yourself rooted in the earth just before opening your eyes helps ground you.

Finally, I would like to emphasize your merger with the chakras. Merger means becoming one with the chakra energy. For example, merging with the root chakra would involve a visualization of the earth and then of you becoming a part of the earth. It is as if you go inside the earth and feel its properties. Then you merge with the earth. This doesn't mean that you begin to look like a rock! It means that you become the stillness and strength of earth. You feel those attributes within yourself. By internalizing the properties of each chakra you become one with the universe.

Transformational Meditation

Bicycle Meditation

HOW THE CHAKRA MEDITATION IS USED

What is the usefulness of the Chakra Meditation? This question is best answered by direct experience, so let's do another meditation. This one is called the Bicycle Meditation.

Bicycle Meditation:

Do the Chakra Meditation, but this time place an image of a bicycle in front of you and carry it along, integrating it with each chakra. Don't forget to return by bringing the energies back down through the chakras... What happened?

With a little practice you'll find that the object changes as it is taken into and through the chakras. The bicycle may have started out as a nice, red two-wheeler that you had as a child. But by the time it got to the throat chakra it could have transformed into something entirely different, such as a feeling of rapid movement. At the brow or crown chakra, its physical form probably disappeared entirely.

What happened is that the bicycle transformed from its physical components into its spiritual aspects. In the crown chakra the bicycle becomes the universal essence of transportation. It might appear as pure movement without any physical form. A transformation occurred from a root chakra physical bicycle to a crown chakra essence bicycle. Interesting isn't it?

As you bring the bicycle upwards through the chakras, a discovery process occurs. You begin to understand the bicycle in its earth, water, fire, air, space, mental, and universal aspects. You know a bicycle better now. When you brought the bicycle down through the chakras an integration occurred. The highest essence of the bicycle was integrated into the aspect of each chakra. You may feel a new freedom of movement now because you have integrated the value of a bicycle into your system. Sound far fetched? How do you feel? I'll bet you feel much better now than before the Bicycle Meditation. Practice again, perhaps with a different object.

If you are having trouble relating to a bicycle as you move it through your chakras, try observing it without need to understand what is happening. This process is highly interactive as it uses your internal senses, and will take some getting used to. Each person senses the transformation differently. Some visually-oriented people will see it change. Others may feel the transformation at an inner level. Don't try to figure it out. Simply be the observer. Understanding happens at a superconscious level in this meditation, and there is often no conscious comprehension. The outcome is that you understand a bicycle better than you ever have before! Don't be surprised if your new knowledge about transportation soon comes in handy.

Keep on with this meditation until you're comfortable with your own unique way of sensing the transformation process. It's like reading different books about playing tennis. Until you actually pick up a tennis racket, march out onto the tennis court, and play, you do not know how to play tennis. Unless you move the energies back down through the chakras you lack the complete ability to use the information.

Problem Solving Meditation

Now you're ready for more significant transformations. **Do the Bicycle Meditation but instead of the bicycle take a problem you are currently experiencing up and down through the chakras.**

What happened?

Many meditation students say they cannot remember the problem after the meditation is finished. Others have said that an answer to the problem came to them. Still others have said they don't know what happened but somehow they feel better about the problem. In all cases movement was experienced. Sometimes the movement is subtle, but it is always there.

If the problem has disappeared, great! Problem solved! Be careful not to worry about it so much that it remanifests in your life. Bless it. It's gone! If an answer appeared during (or shortly after) the meditation, implement it. Your wise superconscious mind has spoken. If nothing specific seemed to occur, don't worry. Some problems need time and you have instigated the process of solution. Feel the joy of knowing that the problem is being solved.

You now have a meditative process that you can use to understand or solve any problem that may crop up in your life. This is what was meant when I said meditation was a transformation process. But are there side effects? The answer is yes, and they are no different than those that accompany any other change in your life. There are wonderful ways that you can cope with them. Let's look into those ways now.

Transformational Meditation

Handling Transformations

HANDLING TRANSFORMATIONS

Let's look once again at the meditation process. A Chakra Meditation can be used with a problem as its focus. This results in discovery as the problem is taken upward through the chakras. The result or resolution, whether consciously understood or not, is integrated as the energy is brought down through the chakras. At the completion of the meditation a number of things might have occurred:

- The problem went away.
    Hallelujah! It wasn't really a problem after all.
- An answer or plan resulted.
    Great! This gives you something to work on.
- The problem was replaced by another problem.
    Finally! You actually got to the real problem. What you thought was the problem was only a symptom.
- The problem still seems present but you feel more comfortable about it.
    Good! Now examine your motives.
    Do you really want to solve the problem?
- Nothing seemed to happen.
    That's OK too! Either you consciously missed what happened or the timing was not quite right for the solution to be understood.
    Be patient: the solution is in process.
    Resolution and understanding will come.

Remember, even if you think nothing happened, something really did. Sometimes our conscious mind doesn't want to look at the facts. There are many problems that you may not want to solve. Motivation is important. Examine your motives. Your subconscious knows the answer and will implement it under the guidance of the superconscious. Trust in yourself. Keep on keeping on. There are a number of indicators that will give you a feeling about where the problem really lies. These indicators will also help you put together a solution strategy. And, wouldn't you know it, the indicators are in the chakras. Let's look at them.

Solar Plexus

If during or after the meditation there is discomfort in the solar plexus, you need to look at how you feel about and relate to the problem. The solar plexus has to do with introspection, gut feel, how you feel about yourself. Look inside yourself.

Heart

If there is a tightness or discomfort in the heart, then look at how the problem relates to the environment around you. Your friends, family, work, and home are singularly or collectively connected to your problem and how you feel about it. The heart has to do with your relationship to the environment and the environments' relationship to you. Look around yourself.

Throat

If there is a tightness in the throat (sometimes coughing, etc.), then look at your communication pattern. Should you speak to someone about the problem? What is it that you are afraid to divulge to others? What are you keeping to yourself? Why are you reluctant to discuss the problem?

Brow (Head)

If you get a headache, relax. You are consciously (intellectually) pursuing the problem too intensely. Let go of the details or preconceived notions you may have as to how the problem should be solved. You may be avoiding communication or putting it off until the last possible moment. Become quiet and let the superconscious work. Put the problem aside and have some fun.

In general, if you find a chakra reacting or becoming uncomfortable during your meditation, move back down at least one chakra (two if possible). Then gently move upward again to the chakra that is causing the discomfort. This is common with the solar plexus, the heart, and the throat. Your chakras speak to you on physical levels. Listen to them.

If problems stay around long enough they will eventually find a home in your physical body. It is not unusual to become congested while you are working on particularly difficult problems. This means that the blockage is breaking up at physical levels and is being naturally removed. As you handle the problem the physical anomaly will disappear or, in many cases, break up into fluids that can be flushed out by the normal process of elimination. In some cases you might find that you have hot flashes or that you run a slight fever. Often you will get a cold or a dripping nose, or your sinuses will drain. What is happening here is that unneeded aspects within yourself are literally being burned and flushed away. It is important to drink lots of water. Plain water, not tea, juices, etc.; the purer the water the better.

Overcoming Sadness

Sometimes I become sad or feel a sense of loss or emptiness when I have solved a problem. This is due to the fact that I have eliminated an aspect of myself that has been around for some time. It is like losing a friend, even if the friend was not a good one. This is a common situation and if this happens to you, here is a process that works extremely well for releasing the sadness.

First, firmly decide that you want to eliminate the sadness. Some people want to grieve or stay depressed for awhile. A day or so is long enough. If a great deal of time transpires, the emotion starts to establish itself as dis-ease in the body. Or a new problem will start becoming established. Tell yourself that you deserve to be happy. After all, you just solved the problem, didn't you?

Next, find the location of the sadness within your body. Likely places to look are in the solar plexus, heart, or throat. However, it could be anywhere.

Then, define the emotions shape. Is it round? Is it like a football?

Next, define its size. Is it the size of a pea? An orange? The world?

Good. You have defined its position, shape, and size. Now think of the happiest moment that you can remember experiencing in this lifetime. (Past lives do not count.) It is important to stay in the present. Feel the joy of that moment.

Finally take that joy and fill the sad space you just discovered with it. Feel joy move into that place and fill it completely. Feel the joy expand beyond there, filling your entire body, pulsating and swirling, touching you from your toes to your fingertips and everywhere in between. See the joy expand beyond you to touch all aspects of your environment. That's it. Congratulations. You have filled emptiness with joy. Who could ask for more.

Establishing Proper Thoughts

It is important to handle negative thoughts, embarrassments, anger, and any other unwanted emotion as soon as possible. Many such thoughts and feelings result from your past experiences and will have introduced blockages into your system. The blockages eventually need to be removed if you are to allow timely growth and gentle transformation into your life.

In the brow chakra description I went over how the mind is the instigator of all manifestation in our lives. Good thoughts manifest desirable experiences. Bad thoughts manifest negative experiences. Be aware of your thoughts. **If you find yourself thinking something that you don't want to see come to fruition (for instance, the thought "Boy, am I stupid!"), cancel it then and there by firmly saying out loud or to yourself, "cancel, cancel, cancel!" Immediately see yourself as a wise person who understands great truths. Literally see yourself as an intelligent and wise person!** Your subconscious responds to this positive thought and effectively erases the undesirable one. The visualization should be the opposite of the negative thought. You are replacing a negative with a positive.

Handling Embarrassments

From time to time I have noticed embarrassments from the past just popping into my mind. This causes me to relive the situation and to reexperience the embarrassment. A favorite that haunted me for years happened at my high school senior prom. My date was a cute red-headed girl that I had wanted to see for some time, and the prom was our first date. It seemed that every time we danced I stepped on her foot at least once. What an embarrassing night! Even thirty years later, that evening would randomly resurrect itself in my mind. Later, after I had removed that embarrassment from my subconscious, I found that I could once again enjoy dancing. I realized then that I had not danced for years simply because the old embarrassment had blocked me from participating. I finally realized the release and enjoyment that dancing had to offer. I opened up a part of my life that had not known joy for over thirty years.

The process that I used to eliminate the dancing embarrassment, as well as many many others, is simple:

First, clearly bring the situation to your mind. Don't worry about reestablishing the situation stronger than before. Recognition or remembrance of the event is important. It is difficult to eliminate

situations that you suppress. Clearly seeing the embarrassment eliminates suppression. See the event and all the people that were a part of it below you, as if you are the director of a play and you are sitting in the balcony.

Next, see the entire scene flooded in brilliant light. From the perspective of the balcony, allow yourself to see the growth and good that has come from the situation. The growth is always there and from your high perspective you will be able to see it without experiencing personal pain. Often you will see humor in the situation. Humor is beneficial because laughter provides a healing release.

Then, bless and forgive everyone who was a part of the situation, including yourself. Forgiving yourself is particularly important. The act of forgiveness allows the final release.

Finally, feel within yourself the fulfillment that comes from the elimination of something that has limited your growth.

That's it. This short and simple four-step process will help you establish a firm foundation for greater and greater growth. This process is also helpful for removing grief and guilt. It is best used at the instant the embarrassing moment comes into your mind. You do not need to go into a deep meditation. A quiet five minutes is all it takes.

Handling Anger

The source of all anger rests in insecurity. You are never really angry at something outside yourself, you are angry at something inside yourself. The external event that you thought was the cause of anger is really a mirror of something within yourself. You are insecure about something and you don't like it. Sound far fetched? Well, examine a few times when you were angry recently and look for the insecurity. It will always be there.

When you recognize your insecurity, the transformation is more than half over. You can use the Problem Solving Meditation with that insecurity as its focus and allow meditative wisdom to provide you with a greater understanding. You will find a renewed strength in handling your insecurity and your anger. Going after inner weaknesses releases the anger.

While we are on this subject, have you noticed a time in the past when you were passionate about an issue or point of view that later you did not care about? Initially, every time the issue was presented you had to get up on a soapbox and loudly expound your point of view. Then one day the issue was no longer important. You were perfectly happy with someone else's view, even though it differed from yours. What was happening during your passionate period was that you were not only trying to convince those around you about your point of view, you were trying to convince yourself that you were right. Eventually you got to the real truth of the matter and were then comfortable with others' points of view. Truth transforms wasted energy into inner strength.

Timing

The methods that we've just described have to do with thoughts and activities that you no longer want or need in your life. They all involve the clear perception of the situation, the transformation of the situation, and the recognition of transformation. The instant in which you recognize the need for transformation is extremely important. That instant can come weeks or years after the event, or it can come the moment before the event happens. The sooner the detrimental situation is recognized the better.

Initially you may find that you reexperience or remember many detrimental events from the past. Once those are transformed, you begin to discover most events immediately after the event has occurred. Finally, you will be able to transform the thought process at the instant it comes into your mind. This signals that you are beginning to operate using the superconscious mind and no longer have the need for detrimental events in your life.

Congratulations! Eventually you will have no detrimental thoughts or emotions.

Now you have a set of meditations and processes that can change your life for the better through the elimination and transformation of problems. Take this process seriously. It works! I don't mean walk around in a serious mood. I mean accepting it as a way of life. You are on your way to becoming a lighter and more spiritually aware person. You are on your way to really getting to know yourself and to love what you see. You no longer need to be unhappy!

Transformational Meditation

The Nine Chakras

CAN I GO HIGHER?

Can you go higher? Can you reach further? Of course you can. Meditation brings a continual unfoldment of consciousness. It doesn't matter where you have been or how high an energy you have experienced, there is always a greater point to reach. There is always a grander place to go. There is no limit to growth. There is no limit to transformation. You see, life is a spiral. You gain experience at the level that is best for you at the time. Later, sometimes much later, a similar pattern emerges. A new understanding is needed and a new experience results. You have completed a loop in the evolutionary spiral within yourself. You now will have an opportunity to gain experience at a higher level of understanding. If you choose to accept the opportunity, a greater form of growth will result.

Meditation is the same way. If your aim is to grow and to allow transformation to unfold, meditation will be a continually renewing experience. You will find that once you reach one level of understanding something happens to bring your meditation to new and finer levels of understanding. Meditation is a catalyst for your journey on your evolutionary spiral. As you establish a need to reach higher, meditation will be the vehicle to take you there.

I'm about to describe the next step that can be taken in your chakra meditations. But first I would like to say that moving to this next plateau will provide no permanent growth until you have studied, practiced, and experienced the primary chakra meditations. There is no danger in reaching higher. However, if you reach too soon, before integrating and balancing the first seven chakras, the higher energies simply will not have a profound effect.

Never abandon the preceding meditations. Each has its own purpose and capacity for transformation. I start my personal meditations with the first Balancing Meditation given in this book, followed by the basic Chakra Meditation. I find that this practice gives me the balance and introspection needed to experience wherever else I may go in my meditation.

Eighth and Ninth Chakras

There are two chakras that have no representation in the physical body. They are beyond the physical world and conscious understanding. They are called the astral chakra and the white plateau chakra. Both of these chakras are considerably higher in energy than the basic seven chakras. Without proper use they can leave you quite spacy. This makes it even more necessary to integrate your experience on the way back down through all the chakras. Integration gives you the foundation for growth. Here are the next two chakras.

Transformational Meditation

The Astral Chakra

The Astral Chakra

The eighth chakra is called the astral chakra. It resides just beyond the greatest reach of your outstretched fingers directly over your head. If you sit down and stretch your hand as far above your head as you can reach, the astral chakra will be just a bit higher. The color of the astral chakra is gold, and it corresponds to the elemental aspects of formation.

To get to the astral chakra, **go through the first seven chakras and then envision yourself enclosed in a golden, egg-shaped cocoon. Rise gently and slowly above the crown chakra, bathed in the beautiful golden light of your cocoon, until you are hovering beyond the limits of your physical body. The energy of the astral chakra makes it possible to barely perceive the earth below. The features may be blurred, but there is a sense that the earth is beneath you. This is a place where thought forms exist before they manifest as objects or spoken communication. There is no danger. You are wrapped in a protective golden egg, and you are observing the astral world from within its safety.**

It is wise to use the golden egg as you enter the astral chakra because there is a considerable energy shift as you move beyond the crown chakra. The egg softens that movement. In the astral chakra you are literally out of your body. It may take a bit of getting used to.

Transformational Meditation

The White Plateau Chakra

White Plateau Chakra

The ninth chakra is called the white plateau chakra. Its color is a brilliant white, and its elemental aspect is essence. You reach it **by looking up from the astral and seeing, or sensing, a great brilliant whiteness above you. You go up, up, up... higher and higher... until you feel yourself engulfed in that white light. In the white plateau chakra there is initially no movement or sensation other than a great sense of elevation and expansion. There can be a feeling of being at home there.** The white plateau is your real home. It is where you go in between earthly lives.

After some practice, as you become accustomed to the white plateau energy, you may begin to feel impressions and colors. This is the place where spiritual-level teachings are received. It is where your spiritual guides and guardians reside. They can be contacted at this etheric level. It is a good place to go for inner answers. This is the place where all knowledge exists and can be found. This is also the place where knowledge can only be received and understood inwardly. The white plateau is so far beyond your conscious mind that you may not remember what transpires while you are there. Know that the subconscious retains it all. It will release the information as it is needed.

Nine Chakra Meditation

Meditating with the eighth and ninth chakras is similar to meditating with the first seven chakras. The difference is that you go all the way through nine steps or chakras to the white plateau. Less conscious-level interaction will occur. Remember to touch the energy of every chakra on the way up as well as on the way down. The Problem Solving Meditation is particularly effective using all nine chakras because the personality drops away. Nothing will stand in the way of your achieving pure love and wisdom.

Transformational Meditation

Self Transformation

WHAT'S NEXT?

You now have all the tools necessary for a tremendous expansion of your consciousness. You will find that the meditations introduced here -- Balancing, Forest, Seven or Nine Chakra, and Problem Solving (or Bicycle) Meditations -- will serve most of your meditation needs. In addition, the processes for changing thinking patterns and eliminating sadness, small embarrassments, and anger will help you deal with the transformation that the meditation brings.

As you work with these meditations you will undoubtedly make subtle adjustments to your meditation pattern. Eventually you will discover or evolve new forms of meditation or new processes to assist your changing consciousness. These new forms originate from your superconscious mind. As they appear, work with them and refine them until they are comfortable for you. This evolution will be instrumental in continuing your growth. These discoveries are fine tuning for you and meant for your personal use. Please don't ignore them.

Your future path is determined by your willingness to grow, your resolve to meditate, and your acceptance of the transformation that occurs. You are on a path of self-enlightenment that is uniquely appropriate for this new age we are in. You are your own best teacher. Within you lie all the answers.

You have entered a path of joy. When all blockages, angers, embarrassments, unneeded structures, and deterministic ideas are eliminated, only joy remains. When the constrictions of sadness, old ideas, and emotions are removed, only expansion remains. Meditate upon those things. You are in the hands of the greatest teacher the universe has to offer: your highest consciousness. Go for it!

I would like to share one final meditation with you. It uses the Problem Solving Meditation (seven or nine chakras -- your choice).

Bring into your consciousness the most loving experience you can think of that you have actually experienced. It could be a birthday party as a young child. It could be a loving reunion with an old friend. It could be a special moment with your child. Or it could be the unbounded love of a small wiggly puppy. You have had many loving experiences. Pick the most joyous and loving one.

Focus on the love. When you feel it fully, move it through all chakras starting in the root chakra and finishing in either the crown or white plateau chakra, as you wish. Allow yourself to discover a new aspect of love at each chakra. Allow yourself

to feel love at every level you pass through. Spend some time with the love at the highest chakra you go to.

Allow each component of joy and love to be felt and integrated within you as you move back down through each chakra to the root chakra. Allow joy to penetrate all aspects of your being. Allow joy to heal all wounds, both physical and emotional. Allow yourself to experience the unbounded joy that is within you. You are a great person. You are unique and no one else can experience your unique beauty the same way you can. Let it touch everything that you touch. Let it become your Way and your direction.

After you have integrated joy by bringing its energy down through all your chakras, feel the density and comfort of the earth. Take a deep breath and return to ordinary consciousness, knowing that the joy is yours and will stay with you as long as you want it to.

You have discovered all aspects of love and have integrated all aspects of joy. Where you go from here is completely under your own guidance and control. You can't loose. Bless you.

Tape cassettes of the meditations found in this book are available for $8.95 each.

Cassette 1 has the Forest Meditation and the Seven Chakra Meditation.

Cassette 2 has the Nine Chakra Meditation and the Chakra Meditation for solving and handling problems.

The illustrations found in this book are also available as Cibachrome prints. Cibachrome is known for its color richness and longevity.

Prices for the prints are $9.95 for 8"x10", $19.95 for 11"x14", and $39.95 for 16"x20".

Orders and payment can be sent to Altan Publishers
103 University Ave.
Los Gatos, CA 95030
(408) 395-0620

Please include $2.00 for shipping and handling. California residents also include 7.25% tax.

Be sure to include the name of the tape and the page number of the illustration.